Teambuilding Activities Handbook

36 Engaging Activities for Every Group

ISBN-13: 979-8-30020-463-1

Teambuilding Activities Handbook

36 Engaging Activities for Every Group

Jason A. Singh

Table of Contents

Introduction vi

About the Author vii

How to Interpret Key Details...viii

Skittles Ice Breaker 10

Paper Airplanes...12

Bean Bag Pass 14

Human Knot 16

Silent Line 18

Hula Hoop Pass 20

Heartbeat..22

Egg Drop (prep required)..24

Metre Stick Rise 26

Group Story 28

Blindfold Walk (prep required)..30

Back-to-Back 32

You are a Star (prep required) 34

Rock Paper Scissors Championship...36

Three in Common 38

Stranded on a Deserted Island 40

Jailkeeper...42

Goldeneye...44

The Nightly News (prep required) 46

Guess Who?...48

BINGO – All About Us Edition (prep required)..... 50

Same and Different.................................... 52

Pictionary.................................... 54

Evolution.................................... 57

Land, Water, Air.................................... 60

Two Truths and a Lie.... 62

Silent Ball 64

Who Am I? 66

Who is the Leader?.................................... 68

Marshmallow Challenge (prep required).................................... 70

Electric Fence (prep required) 72

Magic Shoes.................................... 74

Team Boggle 76

The Artist Game.................................... 78

Word Bodies 80

Personality Name Tags (prep required).................................... 82

Teambuilding Activities Handbook

Introduction

If this book has caught your attention, you are likely a facilitator of a team, club, classroom, or any group eager to strengthen the connections amongst your members. You understand that effective teambuilding continues to drive the success of your initiatives. After spending hours searching for "ice breakers" and "top 10 teambuilding activities" on the Internet, you realize there is no easy way to find an activity that meets your objectives and can be conducted without investing too much time and energy.

During the COVID-19 pandemic, I revisited my collection of activities I collected through my experiences working at a camp for youth with Autism Spectrum Disorder, in afterschool programs in what are deemed "priority neighbourhoods" in Toronto, and in a variety of elementary, secondary, and post-secondary schools. What began as an informal and scattered collection has evolved into this practical guide – a resource designed to quickly match your goals with activities that are meaningful, easy to set up, and suitable for the members of your group.

Each activity page has been carefully selected for quick selection, helping you to focus in on what matters to you. The *How to Interpret Key Details* section will help you understand my reasoning for the categories I used to organize the activities, so you can ensure the activities meets your needs.

I hope you receive this book as one you can use when you are out of time, out of ideas, and need a quick reference. I also hope the ideas in this book inspire you to try these activities with your own modifications, as you know your group better than anyone else.

Sometimes, the simplest change can make all the difference.

About the Author

JASON SINGH holds a Master of Education from the Ontario Institute for Studies in Education, University of Toronto, and currently serves as the Director of Education at a private career college in Toronto focused on medical programs that serve the community. With over a decade of experience in educational settings, Jason is passionate about fostering connections and creating equitable environments where individuals can thrive.

His teambuilding journey began early in his career, working with youth from diverse and exceptional backgrounds as a Site Coordinator in the *Beyond 3:30* afterschool program and as a Camp Counselor at Autism Ontario Kids Camp. These experiences taught him the power of building strong relationships through meaningful activities that help unlock individual potential. Now leading a team of over 30 instructors at a medical career college, Jason also serves on alumni committees for two universities, where he continues to build teams and foster connections through engagement and mentorship.

This book reflects his hands-on experience facilitating activities in various settings, from youth programs to seasoned staff in educational institutions, helping groups come together to maximize their collective potential.

Jason has seen firsthand how the right activity can change the dynamics of a group. He wrote this book to share these insights with facilitators everywhere in the form of practical, adaptable activities. Whether you're a seasoned leader or have just recently moved into a facilitator role, this guide offers practical tools and inspiration to help teams leverage their shared strengths.

Jason hopes this will become your go-to resource for teambuilding activities and encourages you to share your experiences with him on his LinkedIn at:

https://www.linkedin.com/in/jason-singh-7a78a198/

How to Interpret Key Details

Prep Required	The facilitator needs to prep in advance for these activities. They would not be feasible for a quick activity - but do not let this deter you!	
Objective	Allows the facilitator to quickly determine if this activity will meet their anticipated needs.	
Ice Breaker	This activity is suitable to allow unacquainted team members to meet each other, learn about each other, and begin to develop camaraderie. If an activity is <u>not</u> identified as an ice breaker, it is best suited for established groups, or is not designed to allow members to learn about each other.	
Learning Areas	*Verbal Communication*	encourages the use of sound and word expression
	Non-Verbal Communication	encourages the use of gestures and mannerisms
	Kinesthetic	involves significant movement
	Leadership	fosters the emergence of leaders to guide other group members
	Problem Solving	encourages the orderly process of discovering solutions
	Creativity	fosters creative expression
	Active Listening or Observation	required for successful outcomes
	Strategy	requires specific techniques for successful outcomes

Instructions	Underlined text is used to allow facilitators to quickly skim pages for key ideas.
Materials Required	Be sure to check these before you start, and use alterations based on available materials.
Follow-Up Questions	Note that these are only suggestions. While some questions are identified as being suitable for individuals or smaller groups, facilitators are welcome to facilitate all questions as: ○ whole group discussions ○ small group discussions ○ partner discussions / writing activities ○ individual personal reflections ○ creative assignments (concept maps, drawings, posters, and so on)
Accessibility Considerations	Considers mobility, motor skills, and socio-emotional competencies. As the exceptionalities of each member varies greatly, be sure to determine how each activity is suited to the needs of your team members.
Physical Distancing Modifications	These modifications are offered as a proactive measure, reminding us to exercise constant vigilance. Also known as social distancing, several guidelines were established during the COVID-19 pandemic between 2020 and 2023 to slow the spread of the virus, including: ✓ the mandatory wearing of face coverings ✓ a minimum of six (6) feet (~ two metres) separation ✓ regular hand washing or sanitizing Please follow your local guidelines to modify activities as required.

Skittles Ice Breaker

Objective: Learn names and interesting details about group members.

Ice Breaker: Yes
Learning Areas: Verbal Communication, Creativity
Duration: Long (>10 minutes)

Instructions:

Seat members in a circle or at desks/tables. Pass around a bag of Skittles with the instructions "Take as many Skittles as you like, but do not eat them yet. Make sure there are enough for everyone in the group." Give no further instructions.

Once everyone has their Skittles, inform members that for each Skittle they took, they need to tell the group a fact or something interesting about them (as well as their name).

Materials Required:

- ✓ Large bag of Skittles
- ✓ Paper towels
- ✓ Hand sanitizer (or a sink) to clean hands (they get sticky!)

Follow-up Questions:

1. How did you decide how many Skittles to take?
2. What is greed? Do you think it is good or bad?
3. What is indulgence? Do you think it is good or bad?

Accessibility Considerations:

- Skittles may be substituted with any other candy or small snack (ensure there are enough for the entire group) based on dietary considerations
- Facilitator can provide suggestions for shy members to share (favorite subject in school, pets, siblings, favorite book, favorite movie, and so on)
- Facilitator can ask follow-up questions (or allow other members to ask) to deepen group interaction

Physical Distancing Modifications:

- Facilitator can distribute Skittles using gloves, or pour them out of the bag onto each member's paper towel (or into their hands) without touching them
- Importance of hand sanitizing and washing hands can be discussed

Paper Airplanes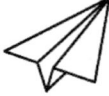

Objective: Learn names and meet other group members.

<u>Ice Breaker</u>: Yes
<u>Learning Areas</u>: Kinesthetic, Verbal Communication
<u>Duration</u>: Long (>10 minutes)

Instructions:

<u>Individually</u>, each member writes their <u>name</u>, something they <u>like</u> and something they <u>dislike</u> on a piece of paper. Once completed, members create a paper airplane using the paper.

Members stand around the space and, <u>on cue</u>, launch their airplanes. For <u>30 seconds</u>, they continuously pick up any airplanes around them and relaunch them.

At the 30 seconds, each member picks up one airplane, then proceeds to <u>find this member</u>.

Once settled, each member will introduce the member they found to the group, including their like and dislike.

Materials Required:

✓ Paper (preferably scrap if available)
✓ Writing utensils (a pencil, pen, marker, or crayon)

Follow-up Questions:

1. [Group] What should we do with all this paper? (ideas of recycling, repurposing)
2. [Pair/Individual] What did you learn about your partner? (can create a writing or visual activity out of responses)

Accessibility Considerations:

- Members may require assistance folding paper airplanes (can also have other members assist [leadership])
- Consider mobility issues with folding and throwing paper airplanes and/or finding the other group member

Physical Distancing Modifications:

➢ It is recommended that this activity takes place <u>outdoors</u>
➢ As an alternative, facilitators can collect the airplanes after they are thrown (or have a few volunteers with gloves do this). After being left untouched for a few days, they can redistribute them to complete the activity of finding the partner and sharing what they learned

Bean Bag Pass

Objective: Learn the names of group members.

Ice Breaker: Yes
Learning Areas: Kinesthetic, Verbal Communication, Active Listening
Duration: Short (<10 minutes)

Instructions:

Stand members in a circle facing the center. Give one member a bean bag. Instruct them to throw it to a member across the circle, saying "Here you go, <name>." The receiver replies, "Thank you, <name>." If a member does not know a person's name, instruct them to ask.

The member throws it to a new person in the group, repeating the same lines.

Extension: Once every member has had the beanbag, the last member can throw it back to the first person. The facilitator can instruct the group to complete the circuit again as fast as possible. This can be repeated to try to beat their own time. As an added challenge, the group can try to do the circuit backwards.

Materials Required:

✓ Bean bag (or another small item that can be easily and harmlessly thrown)

Follow-up Questions:

1. Was it difficult to be polite? (a good prompt if there is group tension)
2. What happened when you were distracted by other things happening in the group?
3. How was the group able to achieve their fastest time? (ideas of teamwork and collaboration)

Accessibility Considerations:

▪ Consider mobility issues with throwing and catching the object

Physical Distancing Modifications:

➤ Members can point at or use a gesture towards each other instead of using a physical object
➤ Members can create a gesture that has a symbolic meaning for the group
➤ Note that keeping attention will be more difficult, as there is not a physical item to track

Human Knot

Objective: "Unknot" the group without releasing hands.

<u>Ice Breaker</u>: No
<u>Learning Areas</u>: Kinesthetic, Problem Solving, Strategy, Leadership
<u>Duration</u>: Short (< 10 minutes)

Instructions:

<u>Divide members into groups of 5-10</u>. Each group will stand in a circle facing their group members.

Instruct each member to reach their <u>right hand</u> into the center of the circle and hold any other member's hand. Next, each member will reach their <u>left hand</u> into the circle and hold a <u>different</u> person's hand.

Finally, instruct each group to untangle themselves <u>without releasing anyone's hands</u>. Once completed, some members will be standing backwards – this is okay!

Materials Required:

✓ None

Follow-up Questions:

1. What strategies did you use to get out of the knot?
2. Did your group have a leader? If so, how were they chosen? If not, would it have made a difference if you had a leader?

Accessibility Considerations:

- Consider mobility issues with holding hands and maneuvering in complex ways (bending, crawling, stretching)

Physical Distancing Modifications:

➢ It is recommended that this activity takes place <u>outdoors</u>
➢ Members can be given rope or string of a certain length and hold another member's string as opposed to their hand. This will create spacing to allow the group to untangle themselves without needing to be too close. The strings can be tied to wrists if holding them is an issue

Silent Line

Objective: Line up according to the given criteria without using verbal communication.

<u>Ice Breaker</u>: Yes/No
<u>Learning Areas</u>: Kinesthetic, Problem Solving, Leadership, Non-Verbal Communication, Active Observation
<u>Duration</u>: Short (< 10 minutes)

Instructions:

<u>Instruct the entire group to arrange themselves in a line based on a set of criteria without speaking</u>. The facilitator should set the acceptable forms of communication at the start of the activity. The most common are gestures and counting on fingers. Some members may try to write things down or use digital devices to communicate. The facilitator should also instruct which side of the line each criterion falls. For example, "tallest on the left side, shortest on the right side."

Once members are finished, start from one side of the line, and determine if the group was successful. For criteria such as birthdays, members can say them out loud. For visual criteria such as height, the facilitator can be the judge.

Criteria:
- Height
- Birthday month and day
- Hair colour (dark to light)
- Eye colour (light to dark)
- Hair length

Note: This activity can be used as an ice breaker if members give the criteria verbally along with their name.

Materials Required:

✓ None

Follow-up Questions:

1. How did you arrange yourself without talking?
2. Did you understand what others were trying to communicate to you? Did they understand you?
3. What other types of communication exist aside from speaking?

Accessibility Considerations:

- Consider mobility issues with walking around the space

Physical Distancing Modifications:

➤ It is recommended that this activity takes place <u>outdoors</u>
➤ Members can space themselves out in the line and when communicating with each other
➤ Additional materials (tape, pylons, and so on) can be used to enforce physical distancing

Hula Hoop Pass

Objective: Return the hula hoop to its starting position without releasing each other's hands.

<u>Ice Breaker</u>: No
<u>Learning Areas</u>: Kinesthetic, Strategy
<u>Duration</u>: Short (< 10 minutes)

Instructions:

<u>Instruct members to stand in a circle, facing each other, holding hands.</u> Break the circle in two places, insert two hula hoops, and have members rejoin hands. Instruct members to pass the hula hoops all the way around the circle <u>without releasing each other's hands</u>.

Materials Required:

✓ Two hula hoops

Follow-up Questions:

1. How were you able to get the hula hoops around the circle?
2. What would happen if someone were to let go?
3. Was this activity easy or difficult? Why?

Accessibility Considerations:

- Consider mobility issues with holding hands and maneuvering the hula hoops (stretching, bending)

Physical Distancing Modifications:

➢ It is recommended that this activity takes place <u>outdoors</u>

Heartbeat

Objective: Pass the heartbeat around the circle as quickly as possible.

Ice Breaker: No
Learning Areas: Kinesthetic, Active Observation, Strategy
Duration: Short (< 10 minutes)

Instructions:

Instruct members to stand in a circle, facing each other, holding hands. Each member will squeeze the hand of the person next to them to simulate a heartbeat. All members will watch the heartbeat be passed around the circle. The facilitator will time a full rotation. This activity can be repeated over multiple days to try to obtain the fastest time. It can also be used in multiple sessions over a long period, and the order of members can change.

Materials Required:

✓ Stopwatch

Follow-up Questions:

1. What do we need to do to get the quickest time possible?
2. What stops the group from performing well?

Accessibility Considerations:

- Consider mobility issues with holding and squeezing hands

Physical Distancing Modifications:

➢ It is recommended that this activity takes place <u>outdoors</u>
➢ Members can be spaced out and use a gesture to pass the heartbeat to each other

Egg Drop
(prep required)

Objective: Design an apparatus that successfully protects an egg from a drop.

Ice Breaker: No
Learning Areas: Problem Solving, Leadership, Creativity, Strategy
Duration: Long (> 10 minutes)

Instructions:

Divide members into groups of 3-5. Give each group the materials listed. Instruct members to use any/all the materials to create an apparatus that will protect the egg from breaking when dropped from a chosen height (commonly 1 meter and 2 meters). No other materials or tools are permitted. Set a reasonable time limit based on the age group.

Next, the facilitator will allow each group to drop their apparatuses in turn, checking each egg after a drop. A successful drop will have a fully intact egg with no cracks or fractures.

Materials Required for <u>each group</u>:

- ✓ 1 raw egg (backup eggs are useful as they can break or be dropped during construction)
- ✓ 10 straws
- ✓ 1 metre of string
- ✓ 1 metre of masking tape
- ✓ 1 plastic cup
- ✓ 2 balloons
- ✓ 1 pair of scissors

Follow-up Questions:

1. [Before each drop] Explain your group's design.
2. [After all drops] Which methods were successful? Why?
3. How did your group decide on your design?

Accessibility Considerations:

- Consider fine motor abilities required to work with the given materials
- Materials can be adjusted based on available resources

Physical Distancing Modifications:

- ➢ If the group is small, each member can build their own apparatus
- ➢ Groups can be assigned roles (designer, builder, and so on) to minimize contact between members while building the apparatus
- ➢ Groups can be distanced during the egg drops and follow-up questions

Metre Stick Rise

Objective: Raise a metre stick into the air collectively as a group.

<u>Ice Breaker</u>: No
<u>Learning Areas</u>: Problem Solving, Verbal Communication, Kinesthetic, Strategy, Leadership

Instructions:

<u>Divide members into groups of 6</u>. Place a metre stick on the ground and instruct group members to stand around it (3 on either side). Each member will <u>crouch</u> and place the metre stick on the <u>index finger of one hand</u>. Once ready, instruct each group to stand upright without dropping the metre stick.

Materials Required:

✓ 1 metre stick per group

Follow-up Questions:

1. Did you have any challenges lifting the metre stick?
2. How did your group successfully lift the stick?

Accessibility Considerations:

- Consider mobility issues with crouching and rising with an outstretched arm
- Can also use any long, rigid object in place of a metre stick (ensure no sharp edges)

Physical Distancing Modifications:

➢ It is recommended that this activity takes place <u>outdoors</u>

Group Story

Objective: Create a story collaboratively as a group.

Ice Breaker: Yes/No
Learning Areas: Verbal Communication, Creativity
Duration: Short (<10 minutes)

Instructions:

Seat members in a circle. Begin with "*Once upon a time, there was a...*", and point at a member to continue. Stop them at a critical moment in their story (ideally before a noun or verb) and point to the next person to continue the story. Continue this process until all members have contributed.

Materials Required:

✓ None

Follow-up Questions:

1. What did you like about our story?
2. When you were stopped, did the next person continue the story in the way you expected?

Accessibility Considerations:

- Consider verbal communication as members each speak with full attention on them

Physical Distancing Modifications:

➢ Seating can be modified to ensure physical distancing

Blindfold Walk
(prep required)

Objective: Successfully guide your partner through the course safely, using only verbal instructions.

Ice Breaker: No – this activity requires established trust
Learning Areas: Verbal Communication, Kinesthetic, Problem Solving, Active Listening, Strategy
Duration: Long (>10 minutes)

Instructions:

Create an obstacle course to walk through, including different textures to walk on, dips and rises, and so on. Divide members into partners. One partner will put on a blindfold. The non-blindfolded partner must verbally instruct the other through the course by walking only, ensuring they avoid obstacles and do not trip. Partners can only make contact if there is a safety issue.

Once completed, partners will switch and do the course in reverse.

Materials Required:

- ✓ Cloths to use as blindfolds
- ✓ Optional: pylons to create the obstacle course

Follow-up Questions:

1. How did it feel to be the one giving instructions? The one blindfolded? Which did you prefer?
2. How do think individuals that have vision impairments may feel in their day-to-day lives?

Accessibility Considerations:

- Consider mobility issues with walking on uneven ground blindfolded
- Consider how this activity will be interpreted by visually impaired members
- If safety is a concern based on physical ability, the blindfolded individual can hold the arm of their partner while being verbally instructed
- Consider the mobility of members and safety of the course in its creation (trip hazards, inclines, and declines, and so on)

Physical Distancing Modifications:

➤ It is recommended that this activity takes place <u>outdoors</u> (creating the obstacle course is much easier!)

Back-to-Back ⇄

Objective: Successfully stand up with your partner or group, without unlinking arms.

<u>Ice Breaker</u>: No
<u>Learning Areas</u>: Kinesthetic, Problem Solving, Verbal Communication, Strategy, Leadership
<u>Duration</u>: Short (<10 minutes)

Instructions:

<u>Divide members into pairs</u>. Have each pair sit back-to-back on the floor. Members reach back and lock both of their arms with their partners' arms at the elbows. Instruct members to stand up together, <u>without unlinking arms</u>.

Once successful, pairs can combine to stand up as a group of 4, 8, and so on.

A time element can also be added to eliminate teams.

Materials Required:

✓ None

Follow-up Questions:

1. What was your strategy for standing up successfully?
2. Did the strategy change when you joined a larger group?

Accessibility Considerations:

- Consider mobility issues with flexibility and the ability to maneuver from a sitting to standing position.

Physical Distancing Modifications:

➤ It is recommended that this activity takes place <u>outdoors</u>

You are a Star
(prep required)

Objective: Give your group members positive reinforcement and receive some in return.

<u>Ice Breaker</u>: Yes/No
<u>Learning Areas</u>: Creativity
<u>Duration</u>: Long (>10 minutes)

Instructions:

<u>Divide members into groups of 6</u>. Facilitators can join in as well! Each group sits in a circle, and each member is given a <u>star template</u>. Members write their names and decorate <u>only the middle</u> of their stars.

Once completed, instruct members to pass the stars around their group clockwise. On <u>one of the five points</u>, write <u>one positive thing about the owner of the star</u>. Once completed, pass clockwise again, and repeat. When the star returns to the owner, all five points will be filled.

<u>Note</u>: Reinforce that only <u>positive</u> things should be written. This activity can be used as an <u>ice breaker</u> by using first impressions (i.e. I like your shoes). In a more established group, can be used to discover more about other group members.

Materials Required:

✓ Five-pointed star template (1 per member)
✓ Markers, pencil crayons, other writing utensils (1 set per group of 6)
✓ Scissors (if you are having members cut out templates)

Follow-up Questions:

1. What is a first impression? Are they important?
2. Are first impressions always correct? Why or why not?
3. What did you learn about yourself?

Accessibility Considerations:

- Facilitator should monitor to ensure only positive messages are being written
- Facilitator can model positive messaging if necessary (Tip: instruct members what to do, rather than give them ideas of what not to do)

Physical Distancing Modifications:

➢ If paper can be safely passed around, consider how to space members out and ensure writing utensils can be adequately divided amongst members

Rock Paper Scissors Championship

Objective: Play rock, paper, scissors while cheering on your peers.

Ice Breaker: No
Learning Areas: Kinesthetic, Strategy
Duration: Short (<10 minutes)

Instructions:

Begin by setting the rules for rock-paper-scissors. Divide members into pairs. Each pair plays traditional rock-paper-scissors. Best of 3 rounds wins.

Members that do not win become the cheering squad for the winner they lost to. The winning member finds a winner from another pair and plays 3 rounds of rock-paper-scissors with them.

In each successive match-up, the cheering squads join the new winners. By the final round, two competitors will remain, each with half the group cheering for them.

Materials Required:

✓ None

Follow-up Questions:

1. How did it feel to win? How did it feel to lose?
2. Did you like cheering for someone, or being cheered on by others? Why?

Accessibility Considerations:

- Consider mobility issues with walking around the space

Physical Distancing Modifications:

➤ It is recommended that this activity takes place <u>outdoors</u>
➤ Members can be lined up to play rather than roaming freely
➤ Members can move through designated areas to maintain distancing
➤ Cheering squads can similarly be spaced out. Facilitators can motivate squads by asking "which team can cheer the loudest?"

Three in Common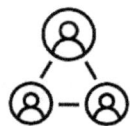

Objective: Learn names and interesting details about group members.

<u>Ice Breaker</u>: Yes
<u>Learning Areas</u>: Verbal Communication, Creativity, Problem Solving, Leadership
<u>Duration</u>: Long (>10 minutes)

Instructions:

<u>Divide members into groups of 3 or more</u>. Instruct members to determine <u>three</u> things they have in common.

Depending on the age group, the facilitator can instruct members not to choose obvious items such as the school or program they are in, physical appearance (eye or hair colour), and so on.

After <u>5-10 minutes</u>, allow each group to present their findings to the larger group.

Materials Required:

✓ None

Follow-up Questions:

1. Ask questions based on their responses (encourage verbal communication)

Accessibility Considerations:

- Consider using heterogeneous groupings
- Can change from 3 things in common to any number as desired

Physical Distancing Modifications:

➢ Members can be spaced out as they interact in their groups and while sharing with the larger group

Stranded on a Deserted Island

Objective: Collectively select five items to bring when stranded on a deserted island.

Ice Breaker: Yes/No
Learning Areas: Problem Solving, Verbal Communication, Leadership, Strategy
Duration: Long (>10 minutes)

Instructions:

Divide members into groups of 4-6. Instruct groups that they have all been stranded on a deserted island and need to determine, as a group, "what five (5) things would the entire group want to have with them to survive for one month?"

Members should be given 5-10 minutes to brainstorm. This can be done verbally or in writing.

Once completed, each group presents their choices to the larger group and explains their reasoning.

Materials Required:

✓ Optional: Chart paper and markers

Follow-up Questions:

1. Why did each group decide on different items to bring?
2. Were any items right or wrong?
3. Which items were the best choices? Why?

Accessibility Considerations:

- Consider heterogeneous groupings

Physical Distancing Modifications:

➤ Each group can be physically distanced, with individuals assigned roles such as scribe, group presenter, and so on

Jailkeeper

Objective: Successfully take the keys without being caught by the jailkeeper.

<u>Ice Breaker</u>: No
<u>Learning Areas</u>: Problem Solving, Non-Verbal Communication, Creativity
<u>Duration</u>: Short (<10 minutes)

Instructions:

<u>Seat members in a circle facing the centre</u>. <u>Select one volunteer</u> to sit in the centre as the jailkeeper. Have the member wear a blindfold and place a set of keys in front of them. Instruct the jailkeeper to <u>point in the direction</u> of a group member they think is trying to take the keys. Talking is <u>not permitted by anyone</u>, but non-verbal communication amongst group members is encouraged.

<u>Silently</u> select a group member as the thief to attempt to take the keys and return to their position in the circle with the keys in hand.

If the jailkeeper points in the (general) direction of the thief, the thief's turn is over, and another is chosen. If the thief successfully returns to their position with the keys, they have the option of replacing the jailkeeper or allowing the jailkeeper to remain in their position.

Materials Required:

- ✓ A set of keys (or any other objects that are noisy when moved)
- ✓ A blindfold

Follow-up Questions:

1. What strategies allowed a thief to be successful?
2. What strategies allowed the jailkeeper to be successful?
3. How did the rest of the group help, or not help, to get the keys?

Accessibility Considerations:

- Consider how this activity will be interpreted by visually impaired members
- The activity can be renamed if the terms "jailkeeper" or "thief" are triggering due to personal experiences or circumstances

Physical Distancing Modifications:

- ➤ Facilitator can create multiple groups to allow for physical distancing when sitting around the circle (or one large, physically distanced group if space permits)

Goldeneye

Objective: Successfully identify the Goldeneye, who tries to remain anonymous.

Ice Breaker: No
Learning Areas: Problem Solving, Non-Verbal Communication, Strategy, Leadership
Duration: Short (<10 minutes)

Instructions:

Seat members in a circle facing the centre. Select one volunteer to step out of the space. Once the volunteer has left the space, select another volunteer to be the Goldeneye. Instruct them to wink or blink at another group member, who must then lie down on their back.

Invite the volunteer back into the space and explain they are trying to determine the identity of the Goldeneye, and that other members will lie down as they are identified. The Goldeneye will try to get as many group members to lay down as possible without being identified by the other volunteer. The number of guesses can be limited.

The round is over once the Goldeneye is identified, or when everyone except the Goldeneye has laid down.

Materials Required:

✓ None

Follow-up Questions:

1. How can we communicate without using words?
2. What did the volunteer look for when trying to identify the Goldeneye?

Accessibility Considerations:

▪ Consider how the activity will be interpreted in communities with gun violence

Physical Distancing Modifications:

➤ Facilitator can create multiple groups to allow for physical distancing when sitting around the circle (or one large, physically distanced group if space permits)

The Nightly News
(prep required)

Objective: Improvise a skit based on a picture from a news article.

Ice Breaker: No
Learning Areas: Verbal Communication, Non-Verbal Communication, Kinesthetic, Creativity
Duration: Long (>10 minutes)

Instructions:

Select an image from a news article. Divide members into groups based on the number of people in the image. Give each group is given the same image and instruct them to create a skit based on what they think is happening in the picture. Skits are usually 1-2 minutes in length.

Give each group 10-15 minutes to prepare their skits, allowing the use of any props available. Once completed, each group will present their skit to the larger group.

Once all groups have presented, share the actual news story associated with the image.

Alternative: Use the headline of an article.

Materials Required:

✓ News article with accompanying image (the image should be made available to each group – projected on a screen is easiest; the news story should <u>not</u> be shared until the end)
✓ Props are optional (can be anything from clothing items to chairs in a room)

Follow-up Questions:

1. Why did each group come up with a different skit based on the exact same picture?
2. Why is it important to read the story and not just look at the image?

Accessibility Considerations:

▪ Consider heterogeneous groupings

Physical Distancing Modifications:

➤ Facilitator can choose an image that allows for physical distancing within the skit
➤ Props are not recommended unless there are enough for each group, and they can be sanitized

Guess Who? (?)

Objective: Determine which member of the other team has the object.

<u>Ice Breaker</u>: No
<u>Learning Areas</u>: Verbal Communication, Problem Solving, Strategy, Active Observation
<u>Duration</u>: Short (<10 minutes)

Instructions:

<u>Divide members into two groups</u>, each making a line, shoulder-to-shoulder, facing the other group. Give the members at the front of each line a <u>small object</u> and allow them to walk up and down the line. All other team members hold their hands out in front of them with their fists closed and facing down (like they are holding an object). The two members walking the line <u>secretly</u> give their object to one of their team members, then return to their place in line. All team members then place their hands behind their backs.

The opposing team has three chances to correctly guess who is holding the object. A point system can be used to track successful guesses, or successful hiding. Once both teams have completed their guesses, a new member is chosen to hand out the object.

Materials Required:

✓ A small, silent object that can be held secretly in members' hands (small plush toy, rubber ball, and so on)

Follow-up Questions:

1. How did your team help you (or not help you) give or receive the item secretly?
2. How did your team decide who on the other team might have the object? What did you look for?

Accessibility Considerations:

▪ Consider mobility issues with making fists and holding hands behind the back

Physical Distancing Modifications:

➢ It is recommended that this activity takes place <u>outdoors</u>
➢ Facilitator can space out members (standing back-to-back creates more difficulty when guessing, but is not required)
➢ Members should sanitize or wash their hands before and after the activity
➢ A non-porous object that can be washed or sanitized between rounds should be used. Alternatively, the object can be changed each round

BINGO – All About Us Edition
(prep required)

Objective: Successfully fill in your BINGO card using other group members' names only once.

<u>Ice Breaker</u>: Yes / No
<u>Learning Areas</u>: Verbal Communication, Kinesthetic
<u>Duration</u>: Long (>10 minutes)

Instructions:

<u>Prior to the activity</u>, collect information about members to place onto a BINGO card. Use a word document or other program to create a <u>chart</u> that will act as your BINGO card. Each space will have one fact, and a blank space to write a name. These need to be <u>printed</u> once ready.

The size of the chart is determined by the size of the group. For example, for 40 members, you may use a 5x5 chart (25 options), while for 10 members you may use a 2x2 or 3x3 chart. The information <u>should apply to multiple people</u>, otherwise it will be difficult to locate a single person in a large group.

Common examples include:

o   Can speak 2 or more languages
o   Has travelled to 3 or more countries
o   Plays an instrument

- o Is on a sports team
- o Can swim
- o Is afraid of heights
- o Can roll their tongue
- o Does gymnastics
- o Is a fan of Harry Potter

During the activity, each member is given a BINGO card and instructed to walk around the space and talk to other members to add names to their BINGO card. Each member's name can only appear on their card once, requiring them to talk to most people within the space.

Materials Required:

- ✓ A printed BINGO card (see sizing in instructions)
- ✓ Writing utensils for each member

Follow-up Questions:

1. [Written reflection] Choose 2-3 group members and explain what you learned about them.

Accessibility Considerations:

- ▪ Consider mobility issues with walking around the space

Physical Distancing Modifications:

- ➢ It is recommended that this activity takes place outdoors
- ➢ The area can be modified to encourage physical distancing while members talk to each other

Same and Different

Objective: Visualize similarities and differences amongst group members.

<u>Ice Breaker</u>: Yes / No
<u>Learning Areas</u>: Kinesthetic, Active Listening
<u>Duration</u>: Short (<10 minutes)

Instructions:

Set a pylon (or any object) <u>in the centre of a circle of members</u>. The facilitator will read a selection of statements to the group. After each question, members move <u>closer to the centre pylon</u> if they agree with the statement, or if it describes them. Otherwise, they will move further away from the centre. If they partially agree, they can move to the corresponding distance from the centre. Encourage members to look around after each statement to see where their peers stand.

Sample statements:
1. I like spiders
2. When I go to an amusement park, I go on all the roller coasters
3. I am planning to go to University or College
4. I have a cell phone

Once initial statements are used, and members understand the activity, use deeper ideas:

5. I enjoy school / this program
6. I feel I am a part of this community
7. I know someone who has passed away
8. I feel safe on my way home
9. I am happy

Materials Required:

✓ Pylons (or any object that is stationary and clearly visible to all members)

Follow-up Questions:

1. Did you relate to anyone you did not expect to?
2. What do you think the purpose of this activity is?

Accessibility Considerations:

- Consider mobility issues with walking to and from the pylons
- Consider mental health in the questions used, given members' experiences and community realities – have mental health supports available if asking deeper questions

Physical Distancing Modifications:

➢ It is recommended that this activity takes place <u>outdoors</u>
➢ <u>Variation</u>: *That's Me*. Members remain seated and distanced. The facilitator reads a statement, and members stand up and say "That's me" if it applies to them.

Pictionary

Objective: Accurately determine what your group members are drawing.

<u>Ice Breaker</u>: No
<u>Learning Areas</u>: Non-Verbal Communication, Creativity, Active Observation
<u>Duration</u>: Short (<10 minutes)

Instructions:

<u>Split members into two groups</u>, each sitting on one side of a board or chart paper, facing it. Each group will send up <u>one person</u> to their half of the board. The facilitator will secretly give both members the <u>same</u> object or action to draw. Begin a countdown timer and instruct both members to draw. The first team to correctly guess what is being drawn wins that round! If the timer runs out, the object or action is revealed. Teams then select a new person to draw. The facilitator can keep score.

Sample items to draw:

o School	o Painting
o Swimming	o Playing a guitar
o Singing	o Playing a video game
o Argument	o Reading a book
o Disney World	o iPhone
o Canada	o Laptop
o Walking a dog	o Lake
o Riding a bike	o Boat
o Crying	o Ocean
o Riding a roller coaster	o Physical distancing
o A Christmas tree	o Bubble tea
o Wearing a mask	o Concert
o Doing homework	o Horseback riding

Materials Required:

✓ A blackboard, whiteboard, or chart paper
✓ Writing utensils for the medium

Follow-up Questions:

1. Was it easier to draw when your group members gave you positive comments such as "keep going!", or negative comments such as "ew, what is that?" or "who taught you how to draw"?

continued ...

2. How did it feel when your group correctly guessed your drawing?
3. How did it feel if your group could not guess your drawing?
4. What is the best way to help others in your group?

Accessibility Considerations:

- Consider fine motor abilities as members have the full attention of their group while drawing

Physical Distancing Modifications:

➢ Members can be seated at a distance from each other while guessing
➢ More than two groups can be used if writing surfaces are available and/or additional facilitators are available

Evolution

Objective: Win rock-paper-scissors matches to evolve into a Queen or King.

Ice Breaker: No
Learning Areas: Kinesthetic, Strategy, Non-Verbal Communication
Duration: Long (>10 minutes)

Instructions:

Begin by setting the rules for rock-paper-scissors. Next, allow members to roam around the space, engaging in a round of rock-paper-scissors when they encounter another person. Everyone begins as an egg. Each member can only interact within their level of evolution (e.g. an egg and a chicken cannot interact). In a round of rock-paper-scissors, the winner evolves to the next level, while the other member devolves to the previous level (an egg remains an egg).

Levels of Evolution

Egg	squats on the floor with their arms wrapped around their legs
Chicken	walks around, bent over, flapping their wings
T-Rex	stands upright, stomps as they walk, and tucks their arms into their chest
Prince/Princess	walks around, waving regally
Queen/King	stands off to one side of the space, posing royally

The round will end when there are no more battles. There will be one egg, chicken, T-Rex, and prince/princess. All other members will be queens and kings.

Materials Required:

✓ None

continued …

Follow-up Questions:

1. Did you have a strategy as you tried to evolve?
2. What is evolution?
3. What did you think about the order of evolution?

Accessibility Considerations:

- Consider mobility issues with squatting, bending, and walking around the space
- The required movements can be adapted based on abilities

Physical Distancing Modifications:

- ➤ It is recommended that this activity takes place <u>outdoors</u>
- ➤ Members can be lined up to play to ensure distances are maintained rather than roaming freely
- ➤ Members can move through designated areas to maintain distancing

Land, Water, Air

Objective: Stay in or move to the correct area based on the instruction given.

<u>Ice Breaker</u>: No
<u>Learning Areas</u>: Kinesthetic, Active Listening
<u>Duration</u>: Short (<10 minutes)

Instructions:

<u>Line members up in a single file</u> behind a <u>marking</u> on the ground, facing the facilitator. The marking can be <u>any straight line</u> that is consistent for all members and not too wide (ex. lines on a gym floor, the separation between carpet and tile, and so on). Explain to members that they are <u>standing on the land</u>. Instruct them to <u>jump in front of the line</u> and inform them that they are now <u>in the water</u>. Finally, instruct them to <u>jump straight up and down</u> and inform them that <u>is the air</u>. Members must jump with two feet (a half jump or a step out of the area they are meant to be in leads to elimination).

The facilitator then yells out either "land", "water" or "air" in any order, at a pace that allows members to keep up. This can be done to move members, or to keep them stationary (e.g. yelling "land" if they are already behind the line). If a member does not perform the correct action (ex. jumps when they should not, jumps forward when they should have jumped straight up, or stays stationary when they should have moved) they are eliminated.

Members that are out can cheer on those that remain. The facilitator can shorten the line as fewer members remain. Continue until a single member remains and declare them the winner! A new round can then be initiated. The facilitator can keep score if desired.

Materials Required:

✓ Any space with a straight line on the floor

Follow-up Questions:

1. Did you find this activity easy or challenging? Why?
2. Why is it important to listen carefully?

Accessibility Considerations:

▪ Consider mobility issues with jumping

Physical Distancing Modifications:

➢ It is recommended that this activity takes place <u>outdoors</u>
➢ Members can be spread out in the line to maintain distancing

Two Truths and a Lie

Objective: Out of three statements each member gives, try to guess which one is a lie.

<u>Ice Breaker</u>: Yes/No
<u>Learning Areas</u>: Verbal Communication, Strategy, Creativity
<u>Duration</u>: Short (<10 minutes)

Instructions:

<u>Seat members in a circle, or in small groups</u>. One person tells the group 3 statements about themself. Two of these are true, while one is a lie. The group then collaboratively chooses which of the statements is a lie.

This activity can be used as an icebreaker to learn about other members, or in an established group to determine how well members know each other.

Materials Required:

✓ None

Follow-up Questions:

1. What type of statement made the best lie?
2. Did anyone's truth surprise you? Why?

Accessibility Considerations:

- Consider verbal communication as members speak with full attention on them
- For shy members, the facilitator can suggest categories such as likes/dislikes, skills, experiences, wishes/dreams, family relations, or random facts

Physical Distancing Modifications:

➢ Seating can be modified to ensure physical distancing

Silent Ball

Objective: Successfully pass a ball between members without making any noise.

<u>Ice Breaker</u>: No
<u>Learning Areas</u>: Kinesthetic, Non-Verbal Communication, Active Observation
<u>Duration</u>: Short (<10 minutes)

Instructions:

<u>Stand members in a circle, facing the centre</u>. Countdown "3, 2, 1, silent" then pass the ball to one member. They throw the ball to another member, and so on.

Members must sit down if they drop the ball, if they make a bad throw, or if they talk or make any noise. The last player standing will begin the next round. The facilitator can keep score if they choose.

If the game progresses slowly, add additional challenges by limiting the time to throw, requiring players to have one hand behind their back, stand on one foot, and so on.

A variation is **silent tree** in which players begin sitting down and need to stand up when they are out. Trees are rooted in place and can re-enter a round if they successfully intercept or deflect a pass.

Materials Required:

✓ A dodgeball (or any other soft object that can be thrown safely)

Follow-up Questions:

1. How did you tell another member you were going to throw the ball to them?
2. How can we communicate to each other without making any sounds?

Accessibility Considerations:

- Consider mobility issues with throwing and catching a ball, as well as other movements based on the challenges added

Physical Distancing Modifications:

➢ It is recommended that this activity takes place <u>outdoors</u>
➢ The spacing of the circle can be modified to allow for physical distancing
➢ The ball can be changed if it makes contact with members' eyes, nose, or mouth

Who Am I?

Objective: Determine your identity based on the answers to questions you ask other members.

Ice Breaker: No
Learning Areas: Kinesthetic, Verbal Communication, Strategy, Problem Solving
Duration: Short (<10 minutes)

Instructions:

Instruct each member to write down one well-known person on a flash card. These can include historical figures, singers, actresses and actors, politicians, or individuals known to the group. (Alternatively, the facilitator can prepare these in advance). Each member then uses tape to stick the card to the back of another member without letting them see it.

Each member finds another to talk to and asks two yes or no questions to try to identify the person on their own card (members can view each other's cards, but not their own). If a member correctly identifies the person on their card, they can take it off their back and be available to answer others' questions. If a member cannot make a successful guess after the two questions, they move onto another person. This continues until they have no more members to talk to, or until they successfully guess the identity.

Adaptation: Instead of well-known people, items that couple together can be written on cards. Examples include peanut butter/jelly, salt/pepper, up/down, left/right, and so on. The activity remains the same, with the additional step that members must find their match.

Materials Required:

✓ Flash cards and tape (or sticky notes)
✓ Writing utensils (unless the facilitator prepares the cards in advance)

Follow-up Questions:

1. What types of questions were the best for determining the identity of your card?
2. What types of questions did you realize did not help?
3. How do we usually categorize things? Why do we choose these categories?

Accessibility Considerations:

- Consider mobility issues with walking around the space

Physical Distancing Modifications:

➢ It is recommended that this activity takes place outdoors
➢ Members can be placed into lines or circles while questioning each other to maintain physical distancing

Who is the Leader?

Objective: An investigator tries to determine who is leading the group in their actions.

Ice Breaker: No
Learning Areas: Kinesthetic, Problem Solving, Strategy, Leadership
Duration: Short (<10 minutes)

Instructions:

Instruct members to stand in a circle facing the centre. Select one member to be the investigator who stands outside the space. Once they have left, select a leader that models a continuous motion that the group follows. The leader should change the motion periodically. Invite the investigator back into the space to the centre of the circle. They have 3 guesses to determine who the leader is. If the investigator is successful, they choose the next investigator and leader. If they are not successful, allow the leader to identify themselves, and instruct them to choose the next investigator and leader in the same manner.

The facilitator can be the leader in the first round to model the activity for the group. Common actions include waving arms, clapping hands, snaping fingers, tapping or rubbing a body part, and so on.

Materials Required:

✓ None

Follow-up Questions:

1. What strategies allowed an investigator to identify the leader?
2. How did some leaders avoid being identified?
3. Why is it important to pay attention to what is happening around you?

Accessibility Considerations:

▪ Consider mobility issues with performing various physical movements

Physical Distancing Modifications:

➢ It is recommended that this activity takes place <u>outdoors</u>
➢ Members can be spaced out around the circle, or split into several smaller groups

Marshmallow Challenge
(prep required)

Objective: Build the tallest structure possible with the materials provided to hold a single marshmallow.

Ice Breaker: No
Learning Areas: Problem Solving, Leadership, Creativity, Strategy
Duration: Long (>10 minutes)

Instructions:

Divide members into groups of 2-5. Provide each group with the materials listed and instruct them to build the tallest structure possible that will support a marshmallow. All groups must start from the same height (for example, the floor) and can only use the materials provided. They can manipulate these materials in any way they want. No additional supporting devices are permitted (propping up against a wall, hanging from another object, and so on).

The marshmallow must be on the very top and must be in its natural form. The facilitator will judge the winner.

Materials Required (per group):

- ✓ 20 sticks of spaghetti
- ✓ One metre of tape
- ✓ One metre of string
- ✓ One marshmallow
- ✓ Additionally: One tape measure for the facilitator

Follow-up Questions:

1. Explain your group's design.
2. Which methods were successful? Why?
3. How did your group decide on your design?

Accessibility Considerations:

- Consider fine motor abilities required to work with the given materials
- Materials can be adjusted based on available resources

Physical Distancing Modifications:

- ➤ If the group is small, each member can build their own apparatus
- ➤ Groups can be assigned roles (designer, builder, and so on) to minimize contact between members while building the apparatus

Electric Fence

(prep required)

Objective: Successfully get each member of your team over the "electric fence".

<u>Ice Breaker</u>: No
<u>Learning Areas</u>: Kinesthetic, Strategy, Verbal Communication, Leadership
<u>Duration</u>: Long (>10 minutes)

Instructions:

<u>Set up a rope or string</u> between two stationary objects at a height of 2-3 feet (can alter based on height of members). <u>Divide members into groups of 4-8</u>. Instruct each team that their members must go over the "electric fence", <u>one-by-one</u>, <u>without touching it</u>. Members <u>cannot go under it</u>.

While members can help each other to get over, they <u>must stay on the other side of the fence once they have successfully reached it</u>. This will always leave the last member to get over on their own.

Materials Required:

✓ A rope or string long enough to be tied between two stationary objects (trees, poles, and so on)

Follow-up Questions:

1. What strategies did you use to get members across the fence?
2. What problems did you encounter?
3. Why is working together important?

Accessibility Considerations:

- Consider mobility issues with stretching, bending, and lifting
- Consider the height of the rope or string based on abilities

Physical Distancing Modifications:

➢ It is recommended that this activity takes place <u>outdoors</u>
➢ Group sizes can be minimized to limit contact
➢ A series of ropes can be used (think laser grid in a security system) to eliminate the need for physical assistance from their team members. Instead, verbal support should be encouraged. In this version, additional prep would be required. The facilitator can also have group members create the pattern of ropes.

Magic Shoes

Objective: Successfully reach the other side of the chasm before the lava engulfs the team.

Ice Breaker: No
Learning Areas: Kinesthetic, Strategy, Problem Solving, Verbal Communication, Leadership
Duration: Long (>10 minutes)

Instructions:

Divide members into groups of 5-8. Designate a line on the ground to represent a cliff and another line 15-20 steps away to represent the other side of the cliff. Instruct the groups that the area between these lines is a chasm. There is a volcano behind them that has just exploded! The lava will take 5-15 minutes to reach the edge of the chasm (choose the time based on the size of the groups). The chasm is too far to jump across, but luckily each team has one pair of magic shoes! These shoes allow them to walk across the chasm.

Each team must safely cross the chasm using the single pair of magic shoes. At least one member must be wearing a magic shoe to cross the chasm in either direction. Shoes cannot be thrown across the chasm.

<u>Facilitator Note</u>: Common strategies include piggybacking, carrying team members across, and using a single magic shoe to hop across, allowing the magic shoes to be passed back and forth.

Materials Required:

- ✓ Optional: A rope or other object to designate the edges of the chasm
- ✓ Optional: 2 objects to represent the magic shoes

Follow-up Questions:

1. What strategies did you use to get members across the chasm?
2. Why is it important to work as a team?

Accessibility Considerations:

- Consider mobility issues with lifting and hopping
- Consider groupings in terms of physical size

Physical Distancing Modifications:

- ➤ It is recommended that this activity takes place <u>outdoors</u>
- ➤ The size of each group can be minimized to limit contact
- ➤ Carrying members can be disallowed to prevent face-to-face contact (hint at piggybacking as a better option if needed)

Team Boggle

Objective: Determine the most words by rearranging the letters in the given word.

<u>Ice Breaker</u>: No
<u>Learning Areas</u>: Verbal Communication, Strategy
<u>Duration</u>: Short (<10 minutes)

Instructions:

<u>Divide members into 2 teams</u>. Each team gathers in front of a whiteboard, blackboard, or other writing surface. Each team <u>chooses one member</u> to come up to the surface and gives them a writing utensil. The facilitator <u>writes a unique word for each team</u> on the surface (can also give each team their word orally, depending on the age group).

The facilitator starts a <u>one-minute timer</u>. Each team needs to rearrange the letters in the given word to form as many new words as possible. No proper nouns are permitted. The member writes down all the possible answers their team yells out to them (it will get loud!).

At the end of the time, the facilitator will go through each word and determine if they are spelled correctly (and if they are real words), then tally the score. Allow the team to erase the board, choose the next member, and begin the next round with new words.

Materials Required:

- ✓ Whiteboard, blackboard, or another erasable surface
- ✓ Writing utensils
- ✓ Eraser or cloth to clean board

Follow-up Questions:

1. Did your team use a strategy to determine possible words?
2. How did vowels help you come up with words?

Accessibility Considerations:

- ▪ Consider the vocabulary and spelling abilities of participants, especially those being called to write on the board (can have pairs go up instead)

Physical Distancing Modifications:

- ➢ Groups can be made smaller to ensure distancing

The Artist Game

Objective: Draw an image using only your partner's descriptions.

<u>Ice Breaker</u>: No
<u>Learning Areas</u>: Verbal Communication, Creativity, Active Listening
<u>Duration</u>: Short (<10 minutes)

Instructions:

<u>Divide members into partners</u>. Provide each pair with a writing surface and writing utensils. Have one partner volunteer to be the artist and the other the instructor. Ask all the artists to <u>cover their eyes</u>. Hold up a piece of paper informing the instructors what the first object is. The artist can open their eyes, and each instructor will tell their artist what to draw <u>without hinting at the actual subject</u>. In other words, the artist <u>does not know what they are drawing</u>. An example of hinting at the object would be telling the artist "it has a brown trunk", "it's found outside growing out of the ground" or "birds live in it" when describing a tree. The facilitator can model this with a volunteer.

After a one-minute warning, allow partners to share their drawings with the larger group, then reveal the object. Instruct members to switch partners and repeat with a different object.

Sample objects:
- o Nature items (tree, flower)
- o Architecture items (school, famous buildings)
- o Indoor items (table, chair, fridge)
- o Transportation (airplane, boat, car)
- o A person known to the group
- o A sport or activity
- o Electronics (cell phone, tablet, drone)

Materials Required:

- ✓ Whiteboard, blackboard, or another erasable surface (can also use paper)
- ✓ Writing utensils
- ✓ Eraser or cloth to clean board

Follow-up Questions:

1. Was it easy or difficult for the instructor to communicate what they were thinking to the artist?
2. Why is it important to make sure everyone in a conversation has the same understanding? What might happen if they do not?

Accessibility Considerations:

- ▪ Consider fine motor skills as members draw out their partner's instructions

Physical Distancing Modifications:

- ➤ Partners can be distanced from other pairs

Word Bodies

Objective: With your team, create the letter or word using only your bodies.

<u>Ice Breaker</u>: No
<u>Learning Areas</u>: Kinesthetic, Creativity, Problem Solving, Verbal Communication, Leadership
<u>Duration</u>: Short (<10 minutes)

Instructions:

<u>Divide members into groups of 5-8.</u> Within each group, <u>choose one leader</u>. Give all groups the same letter or word and instruct them to create it by bending, kneeling, and otherwise manipulating their bodies. The leader provides instructions to the group.

There are two versions to this activity. The first allows members to create the letter or word on the ground, where it can be read by the facilitator standing over them looking downwards. The second allows members to create the letter or word vertically, where it can be read by the facilitator by looking straight ahead (this is more challenging).

Keep words short, considering the number of members in each group. Groups can also be combined for a challenge. The leader can be changed in different rounds. Using a time limit helps keep the game moving.

Materials Required:

✓ None

Follow-up Questions:

1. How easy or difficult was it to follow the leader's instructions?
2. How easy or difficult was it to instruct the group?
3. Which letters were more difficult to create?
4. Why is it important to communicate between each other?

Accessibility Considerations:

- Consider mobility issues with bending, kneeling, and twisting

Physical Distancing Modifications:

➢ It is recommended that this activity takes place <u>outdoors</u>
➢ Group members can each be given a single letter in a word, and spread out from each other to create that word

Personality Name Tags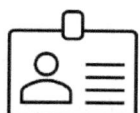
(prep required)

Objective: Create a unique name tag that reflects individual personality.

<u>Ice Breaker</u>: Yes
<u>Learning Areas</u>: Creativity
<u>Duration</u>: Long (>10 minutes)

Instructions:

<u>Seat members individually</u>. Provide each member with a blank name tag and any arts and crafts materials available. In addition to their names, instruct members to add drawings and symbols, list other facts about them, their hobbies, their favorite book/movie/sport and so on.

Materials Required:

- ✓ One blank name tag (can use any recycled paper that can be folded)
- ✓ Writing utensils (markers, pencil crayons, paint with brushes and cups)
- ✓ Arts and crafts materials (glue, foam shapes, feathers, bottlecaps, pipe cleaners, and so on – recycled materials preferred!)

Follow-up Questions:

1. Tell us about your nametag. (Follow-up with questions based on the responses)

Accessibility Considerations:

- Consider fine motor abilities required to work with the given materials

Physical Distancing Modifications:

- ➤ Members can be spaced out as they complete their own nametag
- ➤ Each member can be provided with their own supplies (would require additional prep work)

www.ingramcontent.com/pod-product-compliance
Lightning Source LLC
Chambersburg PA
CBHW070119230526
45472CB00004B/1329